W9-ACR-535

WEST BEND LIBRARY

Popular Rock Superstars of Yesterday and Today
POP ROCK

AC/DC

Aerosmith

The Allman Brothers Band

The Beatles

Billy Joel

Bob Marley and the Wailers

Bruce Springsteen

The Doors

Elton John

The Grateful Dead

Led Zeppelin

Lynyrd Skynyrd

Pink Floyd

Queen

The Rolling Stones

U2

The Who

Billy Joel

Ethan Schlesinger

Mason Crest Publishers

WEST BEND LIBRARY

Billy Joel

FRONTIS Billy Joel is a rarity in the music world. He has been a major player on the music scene for decades.

Produced by 21st Century Publishing and Communications, Inc.

Editorial by Harding House Publishing Services, Inc.

Copyright © 2008 by Mason Crest Publishers. All rights reserved. No part of this publication may be reproduced or transmitted in any form or by any means, electronic or mechanical, including photocopying, recording, taping, or any information storage and retrieval system, without permission from the publisher.

MASON CREST PUBLISHERS INC.
370 Reed Road
Broomall, Pennsylvania 19008
(866) MCP-BOOK (toll free)
www.masoncrest.com

Printed in the United States.

First Printing

9 8 7 6 5 4 3 2 1

Library of Congress Cataloging-in-Publication Data

Schlesinger, Ethan.
    Billy Joel / Ethan Schlesinger.
       p. cm. — (Popular rock superstars of yesterday and today)
    Includes bibliographical references and index.
    Hardback edition: ISBN-13: 978-1-4222-0185-5
    Paperback edition: ISBN-13: 978-1-4222-0315-6
  1. Joel, Billy—Juvenile literature. 2. Rock musicians—United States—Biography—
Juvenile literature. I. Title.
ML3930.J56S35 2008
782.42166092—dc22
[B]   2007019385

Publisher's notes:
- All quotations in this book come from original sources, and contain the spelling and grammatical inconsistencies of the original text.

- The Web sites mentioned in this book were active at the time of publication. The publisher is not responsible for Web sites that have changed their addresses or discontinued operation since the date of publication. The publisher will review and update the Web site addresses each time the book is reprinted.

CONTENTS

YA
782.42166
J591s

ROCK 'N' ROLL TIMELINE

1951
"Rocket 88," considered by many to be the first rock single, is released by Ike Turner.

1952
DJ Alan Freed coins and popularizes the term "Rock and Roll," proclaimes himself the "Father of Rock and Roll," and declares, "Rock and Roll is a river of music that has absorbed many streams: rhythm and blues, jazz, rag time, cowboy songs, country songs, folk songs. All have contributed to the Big Beat."

1955
"Rock Around the Clock" by Bill Haley & His Comets is released; it tops the U.S. charts and becomes wildly popular in Britain, Australia, and Germany.

1967
The Monterey Pop Festival in California kicks off open air rock concerts.

1965
The psychedelic rock band, the Grateful Dead, is formed in San Francisco.

1969
The Woodstock Music and Arts Festival attracts a huge crowd to rural upstate New York.

1969
Tommy, the first rock opera, is released by British rock band The Who.

1970
The Beatles break up.

1971
Jim Morrison, lead singer of The Doors, dies in Paris.

1971
Duane Allman, lead guitarist of the Allman Brothers Band, dies.

1950s   1960s   1970s

1957
Bill Haley tours Europe.

1957
Jerry Lee Lewis and Buddy Holly become the first rock musicians to tour Australia.

1954
Elvis Presley releases the extremely popular single "That's All Right (Mama)."

1961
The first Grammy for Best Rock 'n' Roll Recording is awarded to Chubby Checker for *Let's Twist Again*.

1964
The Beatles make their first visit to America, setting off the British Invasion.

1969
A rock concert held at Altamont Speedway in California is marred by violence.

1969
The Rolling Stones tour America as "The Greatest Rock and Roll Band in the World."

1973
Rolling Stone magazine names Annie Leibovitz chief photographer and "rock 'n' roll photographer;" she follows and photographs rockers Mick Jagger, John Lennon, and others.

1974
Sheer Heart Attack by the British rock band Queen becomes an international success.

1974
"Sweet Home Alabama" by Southern rock band Lynyrd Skynyrd is released and becomes an American anthem.

1987
Billy Joel becomes the first American rock star to perform in the Soviet Union since the construction of the Berlin Wall.

2005
Led Zeppelin is ranked #1 on VH1's list of the 100 Greatest Artists of Hard Rock.

1985
Rock stars perform at Live Aid, a benefit concert to raise money to fight Ethiopian famine.

2005
Many rock groups participate in Live 8, a series of concerts to raise awareness of extreme poverty in Africa.

2003
Led Zeppelin's "Stairway to Heaven" is inducted into the Grammy Hall of Fame.

1980
John Lennon of the Beatles is murdered in New York City.

2000s
Aerosmith's album sales reach 140 million worldwide and the group becomes the bestselling American hard rock band of all time.

2007
Billy Joel become the first person to sing the National Anthem before two Super Bowls.

1975
Tommy, the movie, is released.

1975
Time magazine features Bruce Springsteen on its cover as "Rock's New Sensation."

1995
The Rock and Roll Hall of Fame and Museum opens in Cleveland, Ohio.

1970s   1980s   1990s   2000s

1979
Pink Floyd's *The Wall* is released.

1991
Freddie Mercury, lead vocalist of the British rock group Queen, dies of AIDS.

2004
Elton John receives a Kennedy Center Honor.

1979
The first Grammy for Best Rock Vocal Performance by a Duo or Group is awarded to The Eagles.

2004
Rolling Stone Magazine ranks The Beatles #1 of the 100 Greatest Artists of All Time, and Bob Dylan #2.

1986
The Rolling Stones receive a Grammy Lifetime Achievement Award.

1981
MTV goes on the air.

2006
U2 wins five more Grammys, for a total of 22—the most of any rock artist or group.

1986
The first Rock and Roll Hall of Fame induction ceremony is held; Chuck Berry, Little Richard, Ray Charles, Elvis Presley, and James Brown, are among the first inductees.

1981
For Those About to Rock We Salute You by Australian rock band AC/DC becomes the first hard rock album to reach #1 in the U.S.

2006
Bob Dylan, at age 65, releases *Modern Times* which immediately rises to #1 in the U.S.

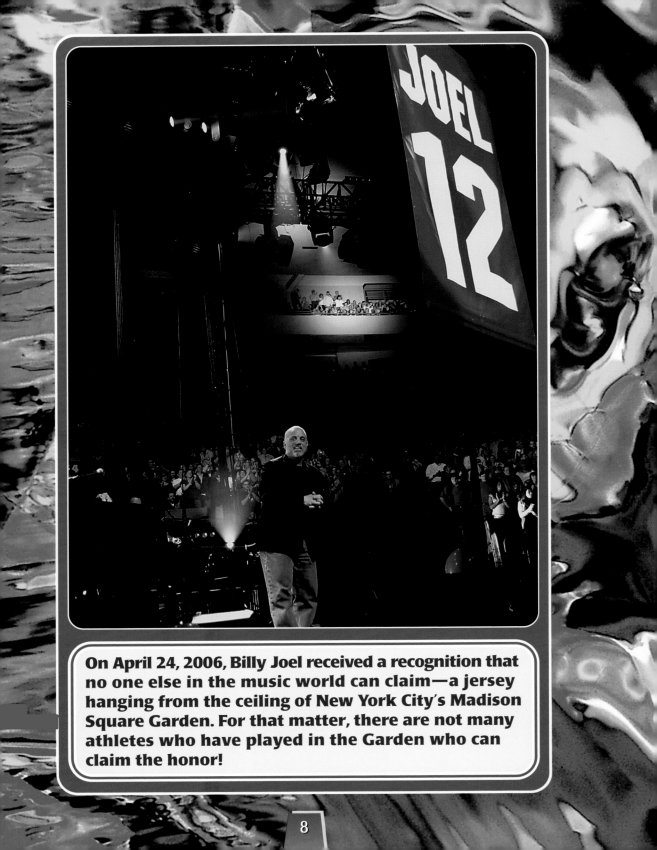

On April 24, 2006, Billy Joel received a recognition that no one else in the music world can claim—a jersey hanging from the ceiling of New York City's Madison Square Garden. For that matter, there are not many athletes who have played in the Garden who can claim the honor!

1

To the Rafters

Since the days of arena rock, musicians—at least the biggest ones—have played concerts in various types of sports **venues**. But never had any other achieved the recognition that Billy Joel did on January 7, 2006. On the first stop of his U.S. tour, he received an honor usually reserved for only the greatest athletes.

As Billy Joel and the huge crowd watched, a hockey-style jersey with the name Joel and the number 12 on it was hoisted to the rafters of the famous sports arena. As it reached the top, the crowd erupted into cheers, applause, and a standing ovation. They, like the Piano Man who stood basking in all the adoration, knew the significance of what was happening.

Making It to the Rafters

For almost as long as organized sports have been around, people have searched for ways to recognize the best of the best. It's only natural; when someone does spectacular things, he or she deserves to be acknowl-edged for those achievements. Sometimes athletes are elected into their particular sport's hall of fame, for example, the Baseball Hall of Fame in Cooperstown, New York, or the Football Hall of Fame in Canton, Ohio.

Another way the accomplishments of athletes who play team sports are recognized is by retiring their number. This means that no other member of that particular team will ever wear that number again. In baseball, the honor is sometimes represented by a painted image of the player's jersey and number on an outfield wall or a display located on the stadium grounds. For basketball and hockey, jerseys are often raised to the rafters, which is what happens at Madison Square Garden.

The Garden

One of the best known arenas in the United States, if not the world, is Madison Square Garden in New York City. Though numerous concerts and other large events are held there, the arena is best known as the home of the New York Knicks of the NBA and the NHL's New York Rangers. Such basketball superstars as Walt Frazier and Bill Bradley have their jerseys hanging from the rafters. Former New York Rangers Mark Messier and Mike Richter also have their jerseys on display.

But it's not just hockey and basketball stars whose accomplish-ments are represented by items hanging from the ceiling of the Madison Square Garden. During tennis tournaments, banners signifying the number of Virginia Slims/Chase championships won are hung in honor of Steffi Graff (5) and Martina Navratolova (10).

Why Billy?

So why is there a jersey hanging from the rafters of New York City's Madison Square Garden in honor of Billy Joel? Sellouts—the good kind. When Billy began his 2006 tour, he accomplished something that no other musician ever had: he sold out Madison Square Garden twelve times. That meant the Garden would be full of fans wanting nothing more than to hear and see him perform—and this happened not one night or even two, but twelve times over the course of his tour.

The words to one of Billy's most famous songs seem to say it all:

"Sing us a song you're the piano man
Sing us a song tonight.
Well we're all in the mood for a melody
And you've got us feeling alright."

Billy's April 24 concert was something special. It was just one of twelve times during his tour that he sold out Madison Square Garden. The sellouts were symbolized by the number 12 on the jersey. Some may find it hard to believe that someone who has been around for as long as Billy has could still draw that many fans.

The only other musician who had come close to Billy's record twelve sellouts was Bruce Springsteen, the Boss. In an interview with the *New York Times*, Billy commented on breaking the Boss's record of ten sellouts at Madison Square Garden, insisting he didn't want fans to forget Springsteen's amazing record. He said, "When [baseball legend] Hank Aaron broke Babe Ruth's [home run] record, it didn't make Babe Ruth chopped liver."

For the fans who might not have known Billy was multi-talented, it probably was a big surprise when the Piano Man became the Guitar Man. Everyone at the Billy Joel Concert and Jersey Unveiling at Madison Square Garden were blown away by Billy's performance. It was easy to see why Billy is still at the top of his game.

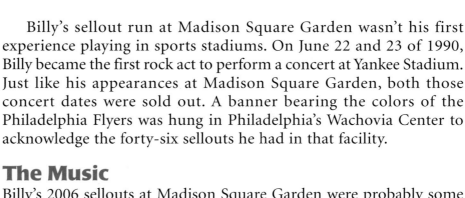

Billy's sellout run at Madison Square Garden wasn't his first experience playing in sports stadiums. On June 22 and 23 of 1990, Billy became the first rock act to perform a concert at Yankee Stadium. Just like his appearances at Madison Square Garden, both those concert dates were sold out. A banner bearing the colors of the Philadelphia Flyers was hung in Philadelphia's Wachovia Center to acknowledge the forty-six sellouts he had in that facility.

The Music

Billy's 2006 sellouts at Madison Square Garden were probably some of the most unlikely ones ever to take place within those walls. He wasn't promoting an album of new material, though recordings from those concerts would be released as a double CD in the summer. No, instead of playing new material, Billy relied on his standards: the songs that had been good to him over his long career, songs that people in the crowd could sing along to. He threw in some songs that people might not have known, but that had been part of his **repertoire** for a long time.

Before the 2006 tour, Billy had been spending a lot of his musical time out of the spotlight. He had decided to slow down, enter a sort of semi-retirement way of life. He had spent much of his career performing, and he felt it was time to rethink his priorities. So Billy worked at composing and recording classical music. He worked on projects with other musicians. He spent time with his daughter, Alexa Ray, who was also interested in a musical career.

Performing before large crowds was not a priority for Billy. The fact that Billy could draw in enough fans to fill Madison Square Garden twelve times, though he'd been out of the recording and performing spotlight for a while, says much about the talent of the musical legend known as "The Piano Man."

Billy Joel's early life was not always happy. His parents' marriage was not a happy one, and when he was young they divorced. His father, a Holocaust survivor, returned to Europe. Though his childhood had its ups and downs, it was something from which he could take inspiration for his writing.

2

The Legend Begins

Helmut Joel was from a very successful family in Germany. Life was good for him until the Nazi regime took over the country. A survivor of the Holocaust, Helmut—now Howard—came to the United States to begin a new life. Part of that new life was becoming a father: his son, William Martin Joel, was born in 1949.

Billy Joel was born in the Bronx, New York, on May 9. Not long afterward, his family moved to Hicksville, Long Island. Family life was not always happy in the Joel household, and when the future music star was still young, his parents divorced. Billy's father decided to return to Europe. Billy has described his relationship with his father:

"I didn't know my dad all that much. He and my mum split when I was pretty young. I really didn't know much about my family until recently."

Finding a Love

Like many mothers, Billy's mother, Rosalind, insisted that her young son take piano lessons. He had always loved all kinds of music, and it only seemed natural for him to learn an instrument. Billy's mother thought he should take piano lessons. So, while other kids were spending their afternoons and weekends playing basketball and stick-ball, going to movies, or just hanging out, Billy was off to his piano lesson or practicing.

Years later Billy recalled his childhood musical education:

"We didn't have a TV, and I'm glad, in a way, because I didn't get hung up on the TV syndrome. We'd see the opera, ballet, . . . everything. A lot of people thought classical music was boring and staid, but I saw the exciting parts, like Tchaikovsky, Rachmaninoff, Chopin. I mean, that's really passionate music. You know, when you're a kid, *Peter and the Wolf*—Wow! That's *Star Wars*!"

No matter how much a kid loves music and might like playing an instrument, the simple fact that he's taking lessons rather than horsing around or playing sports can cause some problems. Billy was not immune to the teasing of his friends. Some of the other kids bullied him, making fun of Billy for taking piano lessons. He even got beaten up occasionally. Tired of being the butt of bullying and fighting, Billy began other lessons—boxing. According to Billy,

"I was drawn to boxing because I got beat up as a kid. I was the kid with the piano books in a New York neighborhood."

Though Billy might have taken up the sport so he could stop being a victim, he quickly found that he was good at boxing. Billy was so good in fact that he became a successful boxer on the Golden Gloves circuit—a series of competitions for amateur boxers.

After twenty-two bouts and a broken nose, Billy's time as a boxer ended. There is, after all, only so much most people will take in the name of a sport!

Like many young kids, Billy's mom wanted him to learn to play an instrument. She must have had a mother's instinct to know that her young son was destined for musical greatness. While his friends were playing sports and hanging out, Billy was hanging with Bach, Beethoven, and the other masters. His choice of "friends" would pay off.

Becoming a Pro

By the time Billy reached his teenage years, he had found two things he was good at: boxing and music. When Billy saw the Beatles on the *Ed Sullivan Show*, he knew what he wanted to be—a professional musician. So he went looking for a group where could take advantage of his many years of piano lessons. When he was fourteen years old, he found one—the Echoes, which later became the Lost Souls. But it wasn't until he was older—sixteen years old—that he found success with another group, the Hassles. This Long Island rock group was a

1968 Sessions

BILLY JOEL & THE HASSLES

A professional musician with a record! With his group Billy Joel & the Hassles, the young musician's career was up and running (Billy is second from the right). Well, kind of. The group released two albums, and both were major flops. Still, Billy did have a recording under his belt, and he was on his way to greatness.

local favorite, and it even released two albums, *The Hassles* in 1967 and *Hour of the Wolf* in 1968 on United Artists.

Becoming a successful rock musician also had a down side. Billy was supposed to graduate from high school in 1967, but as many rock musicians (and their parents) have found, sometimes school and a budding music career are not a great fit. Billy fell one credit short of graduating. Rather than take summer school so he could get his diploma, Billy decided to forgo school and get on with his life as a professional musician.

Unfortunately, both of the Hassles' albums turned out to be flops. In 1969, the group broke up, and Billy and the drummer, Jon Small, started another duo, Atilla. Using only Billy and his skills on the organ and Jon on drums—absolutely no guitars—the duo released a **psychedelic** hard-rock album, *Atilla*. The album was a monumental flop. Not long after the duo formed, Atilla broke up.

Now What?

By 1970, Billy had been part of two failed groups. He had made the decision not to complete high school, so he did not have a diploma either. He found work playing on commercial jingles (including one for Bachman Pretzels that featured the legendary Chubby Checker of "the Twist" fame). He also turned his love of music into a job as a rock critic for the magazine *Changes*.

Despite the fact that he was still working in the music industry, Billy could not beat the deep depression that followed the breakup of Atilla. One potential symptom of depression is suicidal thoughts. Billy had that symptom, and during one dark moment, he drank a bottle of furniture polish. He was rushed to the hospital where doctors saved his life. Billy knew he needed help, and he entered Meadowbrook Hospital. After receiving psychiatric treatment for his condition, Billy left Meadowbrook, better equipped to handle the ups and downs of not just a career in music but of life in general.

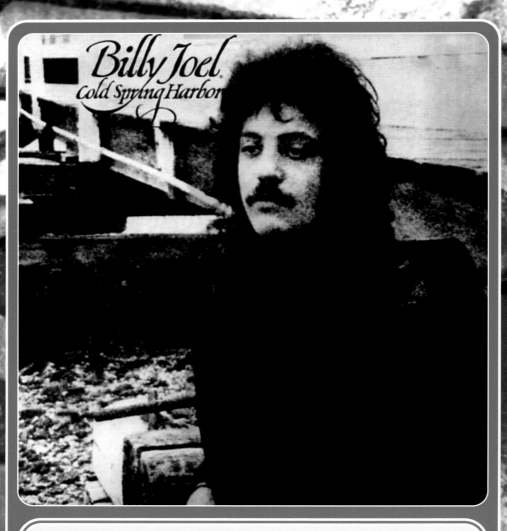

It just didn't work with a group, so Billy Joel took off on his own as a solo artist. At first it seemed as though that career might not get far either. His first solo album, *Cold Spring Harbor*, had technical difficulties the label was not inclined to fix. Billy also learned to read the fine print on the contract.

3

The Piano Man Takes Off

With treatment for depression behind him, Billy left Meadowbrook Hospital ready to try again for a musical career. So far, success had **eluded** the young musician, but Billy was determined to find the key to making it in the music business. Playing as part of a group had not worked out, so Billy decided to go it on his own.

First Steps

Not long after Billy left the hospital, he found a company willing to sign the so-far unproven musician. In 1971, he signed with Family Productions and recorded his first solo album, *Cold Spring Harbor*. According to the Rock and Roll Hall of Fame, Billy wrote his own bio for the albums that went out to music reviewers all over the country:

"After seven years of trying to make it as a rock star, I decided to do what I always wanted to do—write about my own experiences."

This was Billy's big opportunity, and he wanted to make the most of it. But, there was a problem with the album, to put it mildly. A mistake had been made during the **mastering** process: the tape speed was too fast. When the album was played, Billy sounded a lot like Alvin of the famous Alvin and the Chipmunks cartoons and albums! This wasn't how Billy wanted to restart his career.

Family Productions didn't want to scrap the album and re-record it. That would cost the company a lot of money. So that's how the public was introduced to the future music legend. And the album stayed on the market until the 1980s. Billy toured in support of the album, letting audiences discover his true sound. Besides playing cuts from *Cold Spring Harbor*, Billy sometimes broke into a comedy act. The tour received good critical reviews, but Billy wasn't happy with it. He wasn't happy with anything about the Family Productions experience.

Moving On

Billy had entered into his relationship with Family Productions full of hope that this was his opportunity to break into showbiz in a big way. Now, he had an album that should have never been released—and that flopped in a big way. That wasn't the way to kick off a serious music career.

Any hopes Billy had that the record company would want to record a second album were soon dashed. Family Productions was going through serious financial and legal problems. The company did not have the money or the time to spend on Billy, who had yet to prove himself as a recording artist. The best thing to do, Billy thought, was to leave Family Productions and sign with a label better able to help him further his career. Nice thought, rational and probably true. But reality proved to be a little more difficult.

Billy had been very excited to sign with Family Productions—perhaps too excited in **retrospect**. There was a clause in the contract that Billy overlooked in his anxiousness to sign with a label. The contract bound Billy to Family Productions for life! It seemed as

They may be the butt of jokes and bad B movies, but Billy's career was kick-started by a stint as a lounge singer. Starting in the Los Angeles area and then spreading to cover the country, Bill Martin—as Billy was calling himself—was a popular and very successful entertainer.

though he was doomed to spend his entire career—his entire life—tied to Family Productions.

Not sure what to do, Billy and his girlfriend (soon-to-be-wife Elizabeth) moved to Los Angeles, California. Using the name Bill Martin, Billy began playing piano and singing at the Executive Room, a lounge in Los Angeles. He was a popular attraction, and before long, he took his act on the road, playing lounges all over the United States. Finally, Billy was beginning to find some success.

Another Chance at a Record

In 1973, as Billy's career as a lounge act was steady, a Philadelphia radio station began playing "Captain Jack"; the song had been recorded during a live concert appearance. The song became an **underground** hit, earning Billy a following in the Philadelphia area and eventually on much of the East Coast.

The song brought Billy to the attention of some of the major U.S. record labels. Several approached Billy, and for the first time in his career, he could select the one with whom he'd like to record. Billy liked what Columbia Records offered, plus Columbia was an established label (the company dates back to 1888) and thus was not likely to have the same legal and financial difficulties suffered by Family Productions.

Billy's youthful enthusiasm to sign with a record company—Family Productions—almost stopped his Columbia recording career before it got off the ground. He was, after all, committed for life to Family Productions. In the end, however, executives at Family Productions viewed Billy's desire to record with Columbia as a way for them to make some money. There was no doubt that Billy was talented and could be a successful recording artist. The executives realized that probably wasn't going to happen with them, but they were not about to let go of their potential cash cow without compensation. After negotiations, Family Productions agreed to let Billy out of his contract. In return, Columbia would pay the company twenty-five cents for every album sold and put the Family logo on each that Billy released for five years. The arrangement extended into the 1980s.

The Piano Man

Now free to record with Columbia, Billy began work on the songs for the album. He drew from his experiences playing the piano in lounges across America. Released in 1973, *Piano Man* reached #27 on the *Billboard* album charts in 1974. The title single reached as high as #4 on the Adult Contemporary Singles charts. Two other songs from the album, "The Ballad of Billy the Kid" and "You're My Home," also charted.

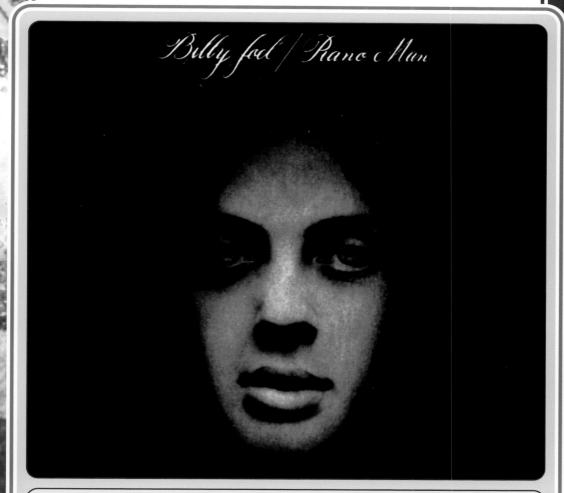

Piano Man, released in 1974, was Billy's first real shot at stardom. The title track drew from Billy's experiences as Bill Martin, traveling around as a piano-playing lounge act. The time spent as Bill Martin paid off when "Piano Man" hit #4 on the singles chart. It was just the first of many hits for Billy.

Overall, reviews of *Piano Man* were favorable; most agreed that the album was better than Billy's earlier attempts. According to *Rolling Stone* magazine,

> **"Recent gigs at a piano bar on the seamy side of L.A. have given him a new perspective and his *Piano Man* reflects a new seriousness and musical flexibility. Its production is reminiscent of Elton John's, and his music has the show-tune ambience of David Ackles. But his ten new tunes also introduce a more mature, less frantic musician."**

After his first Columbia release, Billy followed up the album with a tour that traveled across the United States. He wasn't ready to **headline**, so he and his band opened for established acts like the J. Geils Band and the Doobie Brothers.

Piano Man was certified **gold**, and the album made a lot of money. Unfortunately, not much of it went to Billy. Settling the contract with Family Productions was expensive, and Billy only received about $7,000 from the album's sales.

His first certified hit under his belt, however, Billy turned to a new album. In 1975, Billy had another hit with *Streetlife Serenade*. The album reached #35 on the charts, but most reviewers consider the album weak, not nearly as impressive as *Piano Man.* Returning to his roots as a pianist, Billy included an instrumental song, "The Mexican Connection," on the album.

Certified Superstar

Billy had never been completely happy living in California, so in 1975, he returned to New York. He began work on his next album, but the recording sessions did not go well. Recording the album *Turnstiles* began under the guidance of famed producer James William Guercio. Eventually, Billy fired him and produced the album himself. The album featured songs that paid tribute to New York and life in the city. "New York State of Mind" remains a fan favorite.

Sales of *Turnstiles* were disappointing; the album couldn't break into the top-100 album charts. But Billy was not about to be deterred, and that determination was rewarded with the 1977 album, *The*

Stranger. The album was Billy's first megahit, reaching #2 on the album charts and certified platinum, indicating sales of over a million copies. Reviews were mixed, but most found bright spots on Billy's work, especially the collaboration with legendary producer Phil Ramone. (In 2007, sadly, Phil Ramone is best known as the defendant in a California murder trial.) Ira Mayer wrote in *Rolling Stone*:

A move back to New York returned Billy to a New York state of mind, which he turned into another hit song. *Turnstiles*, which contained "New York State of Mind," was a disappointment, but fans did and still do love that song. It is the anthem of New York City.

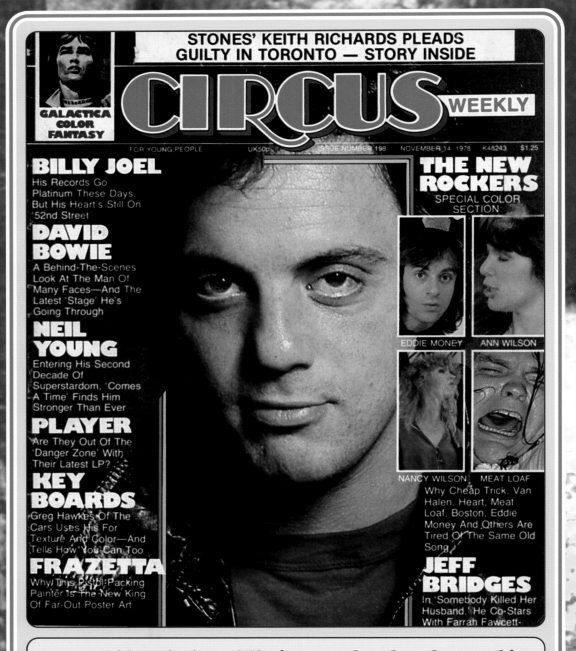

STONES' KEITH RICHARDS PLEADS
GUILTY IN TORONTO — STORY INSIDE

CIRCUS WEEKLY

GALACTICA COLOR FANTASY

FOR YOUNG PEOPLE   UK50p   ISSUE NUMBER 198   NOVEMBER 14 1978   K48243 $1.25

BILLY JOEL
His Records Go
Platinum These Days.
But His Heart's Still On
'52nd Street

DAVID BOWIE
A Behind-The-Scenes
Look At The Man Of
Many Faces—And The
Latest 'Stage' He's
Going Through

NEIL YOUNG
Entering His Second
Decade Of
Superstardom, 'Comes
A Time' Finds Him
Stronger Than Ever

PLAYER
Are They Out Of The
'Danger Zone' With
Their Latest LP?

KEY BOARDS
Greg Hawkes Of The
Cars Uses His For
Texture And Color—And
Tells How You Can Too

FRAZETTA
Why This Pistol-Packing
Painter Is The New King
Of Far-Out Poster Art

THE NEW ROCKERS
SPECIAL COLOR SECTION:

EDDIE MONEY   ANN WILSON

NANCY WILSON   MEAT LOAF
Why Cheap Trick, Van
Halen, Heart, Meat
Loaf, Boston, Eddie
Money And Others Are
Tired Of The Same Old
Song

JEFF BRIDGES
In 'Somebody Killed Her
Husband,' He Co-Stars
With Farrah Fawcett-

Forget gold. In the late 1970s, it seemed as though everything Billy turned out hit platinum, which was the subject of the November 1978 cover story in *Circus Weekly*. Both his albums and his singles shot up the record charts, and it seemed as though Billy's music was being played everywhere.

> **"Together with producer Phil Ramone, Joel has achieved a fluid sound occasionally sparked by a light soul touch. It is a markedly different effect than his pound-it-out-to-the-back-rows concert flash."**

Four songs from the album charted on the top-40 singles list: "Just the Way You Are, "Movin' Out (Anthony's Song)," "She's Always a Woman," and "Only the Good Die Young." One of them, "Just the Way You Are," which Billy wrote for his wife, brought him his first Grammy Awards, 1978's Song of the Year (as songwriter) and Record of the Year, an award he shared with Phil Spector.

Another Album, Another Hit

In a highly competitive field like the music industry, artists are only as good as their latest hit. There's always someone else in the wings eagerly waiting to take another person's place. But those waiting to take over for Billy Joel would have to wait. Billy's next album, *52nd Street*, was an even bigger hit for the Piano Man. Released in 1978, the album became Billy's first to top the album charts; it spent eight weeks as #1. Three of the album's singles—"My Life," "Big Shot," and "Honesty"— received heavy airplay on AM radio, something Billy's previous singles often lacked. The three singles also cracked *Billboard*'s charts: "My Life" at #3, "Big Shot" at #14, and "Honesty" at #24. The Grammys rewarded Billy Joel for *52nd Street.* The album brought 1979 Grammys for Album of the Year and Best Pop Vocal Performance, Male.

Despite the album's success, which proved that Billy was no one-hit wonder, critics were not kind to Billy. He shouldn't have been surprised. He had never garnered overwhelming critical approval no matter how successful a song was. Sometimes the best he could hope for was a lukewarm review from a critic. Reviewer Frank Ahrens wrote in the late 1990s about how critics reviewed Billy:

> **"Many rock critics, on the other hand, have spent their careers despising Joel, giving him, at best, grudging respect as a tunesmith with skills but no ideas. That is, the critics who've deigned to write about him. To the rest, he is simply beneath contempt, a hack schmaltz singer who doesn't have the credibility**

As the seventies came to a close, one thing was certain: Billy Joel had come a long way from his days as lounge player Bill Martin! He had hit records. He had Grammy awards. Billy seemed to have it all—well except for one thing: the respect of the critics.

of even a Neil Diamond. Indeed, the critics' view of Joel is so intensely negative—and some of his songs so unapologetically sentimental—that some fans are embarrassed to admit they like him.**"**

In one famous incident from the 1970s, Billy complained about critics during a performance, even tearing up one critic's reviews.

Staying on Top

Despite the critics' opinions, after *52nd Street* there was no question—Billy Joel was a superstar. The trick would be to see if he could stay on top. As the seventies closed and a new decade dawned, a new trend in music developed. If critics thought Billy's work was "irrelevant" before, how could it stack up against **punk** and **New Wave** music that became popular during the new decade?

In 1980, Billy released *Glass House*, which some historians contend was his attempt to respond to the new music trends. If it was, it worked; the album was his second to top the album charts. Four singles from the album cracked the top-40 singles charts, including the chart-topping "It's Still Rock 'n' Roll to Me." *Glass House* also won another Grammy Award for Billy, 1980's Best Rock Vocal Performance, Male.

Billy released a live album, *Songs in the Attic*, in 1981. Most of the songs had been written and recorded before his first big hit in the late 1970s. Though two of the songs made the top-40 charts, album sales were disappointing compared to his two previous releases.

Billy's next album was delayed by a motorcycle accident. When released, however, Billy experienced something new—critical praise. But sales were disappointing. When *An Innocent Man* was released in 1983, Billy found himself back in the world of multi-platinum sales. The album spun off multiple hit singles, including "Uptown Girls," whose video featured model Christie Brinkley. Billy met Christie in St. Barts, where he had gone to rest after his divorce from Elizabeth. The pair quickly became a couple, marrying in 1985.

An Innocent Man was **vintage** Billy Joel, which meant that fans loved him and critics were not quite so excited. The album brought him another Grammy nod, this time for Album of the Year, but Michael Jackson's *Thriller* took the honor. Regardless, the album showed that Billy was still at the top of his musical game.

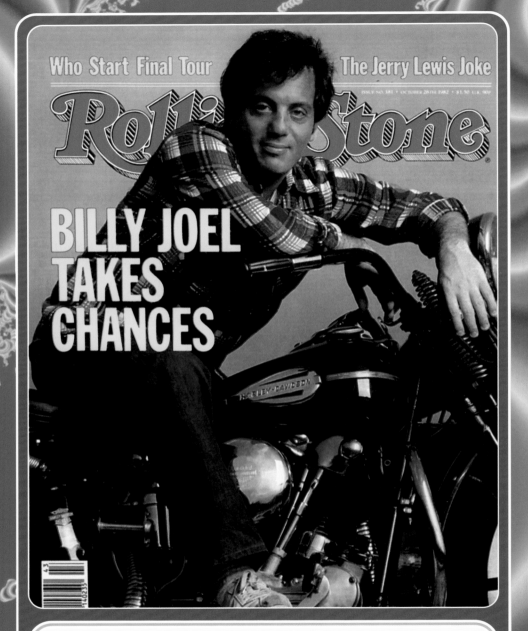

Who Start Final Tour   The Jerry Lewis Joke

ISSUE NO. 381 · OCTOBER 28 OR 1982 · $1.50 U.K. 90p

Rolling Stone

BILLY JOEL TAKES CHANCES

Most music critics just could not understand the Billy Joel phenomenon. At best, most of them had given him mediocre reviews—if they bothered to review his music at all. Still, fans kept coming to Billy's concerts and buying his albums and singles. It didn't matter to them what the critics wrote. They just wanted their Billy.

4

A Change of Pace

The mid-1980s had brought Billy Joel the success and recognition sought by many musicians but achieved by far fewer. Despite having much of his work panned—or just plain ignored—by the critics, Billy had developed a supportive fan base who eagerly awaited his next recording or performance. They didn't care what the critics said; they loved Billy.

There was something about his music that had made him popular ever since he came to national attention after he signed with Columbia Records. Some music historians believed that one of the reasons for his fan popularity was the multiple music styles that influenced his music. According to the Rock and Roll Hall of Fame:

> **"**His classical training and reverence for Broadway musicals have been counterpointed by his early grounding in the Long Island bar-band scene and his love of rhythm & blues, resulting in an enthusiastic yet musically sophisticated approach to rock and roll.**"**

Billy's music also exhibits the influences of Aaron Copland, the "dean of American composers." Among Copland's works are symphonies and the famous ballet *Rodeo*.

Fans of jazz, blues, gospel, and traditional pop music could find their **genres**' influences in Billy's music as well. So could those who liked ska music, a type of music that originated in Jamaica during the 1950s. The genre combined Caribbean **mento** and **calypso** with jazz and the blues. The 1950s also contributed a doo-wop influence to Billy's music. Doo-wop was a style of the blues popular in the fifties and through the sixties. Rather than depending on a musical instrument, doo-wop depended on the talents of the vocalist. With all these influences, it was easy to see how Billy could attract a huge number of fans with **diverse** musical interests.

The Best of the Best

Fans had the opportunity to get a "sampler platter" of Billy's greatest hits in 1985 with the release of *Greatest Hits Vols. 1 and 2*. Columbia had wanted Billy to release a greatest hits album earlier in his career, but the singer had refused; he thought such a release should come at the end of a career. But when Columbia approached him to do so after the overwhelming success of *An Innocent Man*, Billy agreed.

Columbia's instincts were right on target. The four-album, two-CD set was a huge hit. At the time, the collection became the best-selling double album of all time by a solo artist. It came in second to Pink Floyd's *The Wall* for the best-selling double album of all time by a solo artist or a group. In 1999, the Recording Industry Association of America (RIAA), for sales of more than 20 million, certified the album double diamond. As of 2006, *Greatest Hits Vols. 1 and 2* was the sixth-best selling album of all time in the United States.

The album set settled in at #6 on the *Billboard* album charts. Though most of the songs on Billy's *Greatest Hits* had been released on earlier albums, he did include two new songs. "You're Only Human (Second Wind)" cracked the top-10 singles chart, while "The Night Is Still Young" made it into the top-40.

So, if you're Billy Joel, how do you follow up the phenomenal success of *An Innocent Man* and singles like "Keeping the Faith"? You give in to your record label and release a greatest hits collection. *Greatest Hits Vols. 1 and 2* did better than anyone could have expected. In 1999, the collection was certified double diamond!

Billy released a video collection as well in 1985. The two-volume *Video Album* featured all the videos he had recorded since 1977. The set included videos for "You're Only Human (Second Wind)" and "The Night Is Still Young" from the *Greatest Hits* collection. Billy also recorded a video for his very first hit, "Piano Man," and it was included on the video collection as well.

The Hits Keep Coming

Billy ventured into film work with the movie *Ruthless People*, starring Bette Midler, Danny DeVito, and Judge Reinhold. His song "Modern Woman" was a hit from the movie's soundtrack, making it into the top-10 on the singles chart. He included the song on his 1986 album *The Bridge*. This album featured contributions by other artists. For "Baby Grand," the legendary Ray Charles played the piano and sang. Listeners to "Getting Closer" heard Steve Winwood play the organ. Cyndi Lauper provided background vocals on the album as well.

Billy's latest release did not achieve the success of his earlier works, but it did reach #7 on the album charts and sold more than two million copies. For most artists, that would have been enough, but Billy was used to his albums selling double-digit millions. Two of the album's songs did make it into the top-20. "A Matter of Trust," whose video showed Billy playing the guitar rather than his signature piano, reached #10. "This Is the Time" hit the #18 spot. Another song, "Big Man on Mulberry Street," was used as the plot for an episode of the television series *Moonlighting*, which starred Bruce Willis and Cybill Shepherd.

Although most fans would not notice, *The Bridge* also signified a "last" for Billy, and for Columbia. It was the last album that required the Family Productions logo. Finally, Billy was free from the label.

The USSR

In the 1980s, playing in the Soviet Union was almost as bizarre a thought as playing a concert in outer space. To Billy it was a challenge. No American rock artist had played in the country since the Berlin Wall was constructed in the early 1960s, separating East and West Germany. Billy loved history, and the symbolism of playing in the Soviet Union was something that Billy couldn't pass up. In June 1987, Billy, Christie, their daughter Alexa (who had been born on

The legendary Ray Charles helped break down many racial barriers, opening the way for other black musicians. And his talent as a singer and pianist was nothing short of amazing, keeping crowds rocking for decades. In 1986, the two piano virtuosos teamed up for "Baby Grand," which appeared on Billy's album *The Bridge*.

New Year's Day 1986), and the complete Billy Joel band took off for a six-concert tour of the Soviet Union.

Concerts were held in Leningrad, Moscow, and Tbilisi. All the concerts were taped for a future video, and the performances were broadcast worldwide on radio. Billy and his band weren't sure what to expect when they performed. There was no real way to gauge what

Billy broke barriers himself in 1987 when he became the first U.S. rock artist to perform in the Soviet Union since the Berlin Wall was erected in the early 1960s. For Billy the history buff, it was an opportunity too good to pass up. Though the tour lost money for Billy, he believed the experience and symbolism were worth it.

people in the Soviet Union thought about his music. Billy and the others were used to crowds everywhere quickly getting caught up in the energy of his performances, singing the words of the familiar songs, even if they didn't know what they meant. When Billy opened in Moscow, he experienced something he never had before: the audience just sat there. According to some reports, many in the crowd of the Moscow shows were members of the Communist Party who had received tickets to the show from the government. Whether that was the reason the people in the audience took a while to respond, or if they just weren't sure how they were supposed to act, they eventually came around and seemed to appreciate the effort Billy and his band were making for them.

Billy's tour of the Soviet Union didn't go without incident. During a performance in Moscow, he overturned his keyboard. According to the *New York Times*:

> **Some unexpected headlines were made at one concert when, furious with his technical crew, Mr. Joel overturned his electronic piano and broke a microphone stand. . . . Mr. Joel explains that he wanted the television people to stop turning lights on the audience. People at concerts, he insists, like to be in the dark and, in any event, the piano was 'not very expensive.'**

According to Billy, the lighting crew was more concerned about getting the lighting right for recording the concert video than making the audience comfortable.

Though the tour might have had rocky spots, it was a success. The *New York Times* reported:

> **The show's major motif is revealed at the outset. 'We think of the Russians as a monolith,' Mr. Joel said. 'We don't think of them as individuals.' He then begins communicating furiously. During the concerts, he throws himself into the audience, at times being lifted along over spectator heads. In public, he kisses elderly women and gives his St. Christopher medal**

to a young rocker. On television, he tells his adoring audience that 'what's going on in your country now is very much like the 60's in my country.' Partying into the wee hours in Tbilisi, he tells the indefatigable Georgians that he has never been in a place where the people were so warm and hospitable.**"**

Rock's first ambassador to the Soviet Union certainly made an impact. Though Billy reportedly lost more than a million dollars on the tour, he believed it was worth it.

Disney and a Storm Front

After the Soviet Union concert tour, Billy took off much of 1988. He ventured into film again, this time as an actor—kind of—for the Walt Disney production *Oliver and Company*. Billy provided the voice of Dodger in the animated film and recorded "Why Should I Worry?" for the soundtrack. Both his acting and the song were positively received by critics.

In August 1989, Billy fired his manager, Frank Weber, who was also his former brother-in-law. After suspicions circulated that there were accounting problems, an **audit** had been conducted that confirmed there were discrepancies in the financial accounting. Billy filed a 90 million dollar lawsuit against Weber, claiming fraud and that he had not performed his duties appropriately. Not long afterward, Billy was hospitalized for the treatment of kidney stones, and Frank Weber filed a countersuit. Things were not looking good for the Piano Man.

The year's outlook changed for Billy when the single "We Didn't Start the Fire" was released, a sampling of his upcoming album *Storm Front*. The song raced up the charts to the #1 spot. The song is unique as the lyrics are a string of historical facts, rather than the telling of a story. The album reached #1 as well. The album also included "The Downeaster Alexa," which told of the problems faced by Long Island fishermen who had a difficult time making a living.

Getting His Due

Billy followed the release of *Storm Front* with a successful tour of the United States in 1990 and 1991. In 1991, things were quiet for Billy, except for the settlement of his lawsuit against Frank Weber. The court

ISSUE 570 · JANUARY 25th, 1990

Rolling Stone

billy joel

On Fire Again:
The Rolling Stone
Interview

Guitar Heroes:
Jeff Beck
and Stevie Ray
Vaughan

Everyone knows what song lyrics are supposed to do: they tell a story about something—a lost (or found) love, a city, a feeling. Billy proved he was good at writing song lyrics. But he wasn't against trying something different, which he did with "We Didn't Start the Fire," with lyrics that are a list rather than a story.

awarded Billy two million dollars and dismissed Weber's countersuit. But 1991 wasn't only about legal issues for Billy. In December, the Grammy Awards Foundation announced that Billy would be given a Grammy Living Legend Award at the 1992 ceremonies. Joining Billy as Living Legends were renowned record producer Quincy Jones, Johnny Cash, and Aretha Franklin. Billy, the high school dropout, also received an honorary doctorate from Fairfield University in Connecticut in 1991, the first of many.

The remainder of the 1990s were fairly quiet for Billy. He filed another lawsuit, this time against his former lawyer, which was settled out of court. In 1993, Billy released *River of Dreams*. The title cut spent twelve weeks at the #1 spot on the singles charts. The track "Lullabye (Goodnight My Angel)" was written for Alexa, and the album cover featured a painting by Christie. After the tour supporting the album, the Christie Brinkley-Billy Joel marriage ended. The two have remained friends, however.

In 1995, tragedy struck Billy's musical family. Doug Stegmeyer had played bass for Billy on every album from *Turnstiles* to *The Bridge*. In August, to the surprise of almost all who knew him, Doug committed suicide.

The following year, Billy decided to take a break from recording and performing. Instead, he lectured about classical music at colleges all over the country. Then, in 1999, the hall called; that's the Rock and Roll Hall of Fame.

The Rock and Roll Hall of Fame Beckons

In 1999, Billy joined the select few who earn their way into the Rock and Roll Hall of Fame. No matter how good an artist might be, making it into the Rock and Roll Hall of Fame is not a sure bet. First, the artist must meet the strict criteria of the nominating committee to even make it onto the ballot. Then, to be voted into the hall, they must have the most votes and be chosen by more than 50 percent of the voters. Besides Billy, other **inductees** that year included Curtis Mayfield, Paul McCartney, Bruce Springsteen, and the Staple Singers.

Billy was presented for induction by Ray Charles at the ceremonies held at the glamorous Waldorf-Astoria Hotel in New York City. In his acceptance speech, Billy thanked those who had supported him over the years, his life, and his plans for the future:

As the twentieth century came to a close, Billy started getting his props. In this photo from 1999, Don Lenner (left) of Columbia Records Group and Hilary Rosen (right) of the RIAA present Billy with a diamond award. The award signifies that Billy's titles have sold at least 10 million units in the United States.

"It's been a great life. . . . I've had an amazing life, mostly because of rock 'n' roll music. I love all kinds of music. Right now, I'm writing what would be considered romantic mid-19th century classical music."

Billy ended the year—and the century—with a concert titled "The Night of the 2000 Years." Many thought the almost four-hour concert would be his last. They were wrong.

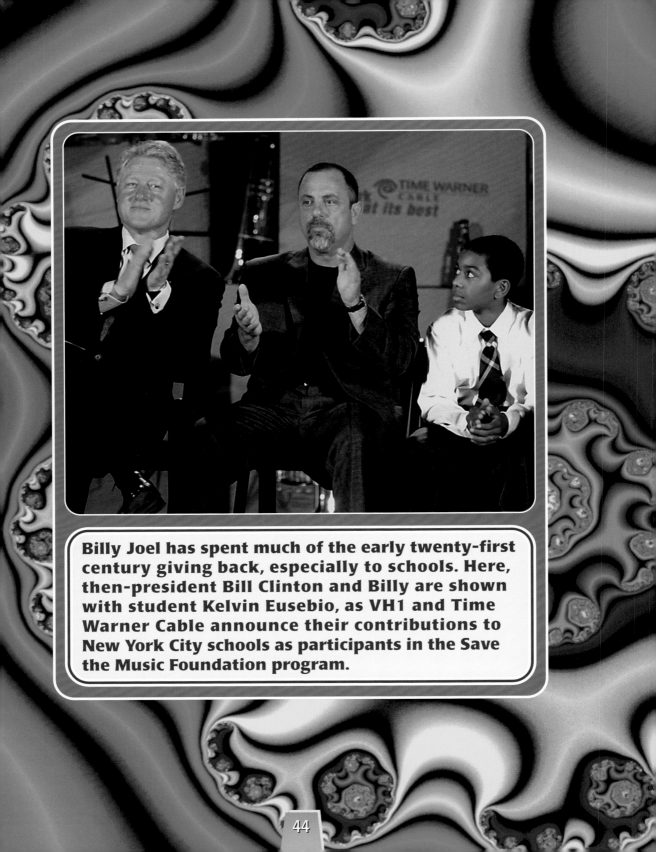

Billy Joel has spent much of the early twenty-first century giving back, especially to schools. Here, then-president Bill Clinton and Billy are shown with student Kelvin Eusebio, as VH1 and Time Warner Cable announce their contributions to New York City schools as participants in the Save the Music Foundation program.

5

Still Making a Mark

As the new millennium began, Billy Joel was a veteran of the music industry. He had spent almost thirty years as a recording artist with Columbia Records. Billy had received the *Billboard* Century Award and been welcomed into the Rock and Roll Hall of Fame. He had also returned to his classical roots as a composer and teacher.

Many wondered whether Billy still had what it took to be a hitmaker. He recorded less frequently, spending time on his other projects. Billy showed that he had time for all of his interests.

Classical Beginnings

Since childhood, Billy had loved the masters of classical music. Such important figures as Beethoven, Bach, and Chopin had influenced him throughout his career. And as he announced during his Rock and Roll Hall of Fame induction, he was composing his own classical-style music.

In 2001, Billy's efforts were ready for the public, and he released the album *Fantasies & Delusions*. Billy composed all of the songs for the instrumental album. But, instead of Billy playing them, pianist Richard Joo performed the works. Like much of his rock music, Billy's first attempt at composing classical music met with mixed responses from the critics. A review by Terry Teachout, which appeared in *Time* magazine, was typical:

> **❝So what's the Piano Man been up to lately? Writing classical music. Billy Joel's latest CD is a collection of 10 pretty solo-piano miniatures with such earnest titles as Invention in C Minor and Fantasy (Film Noir). Unlike Sir Paul McCartney's elephantine blunderings into the concert hall, these pieces are modest in scale, as well as unabashedly romantic, and pianist Richard Joo plays them as if they were spun gold. Alas, they sound like the work of a promising student so in love with Chopin and Liszt that he has yet to find his own voice. A for effort, though.❞**

Despite the mixed reviews, *Fantasies & Delusions* topped the classical album charts.

A Tribute to Heroes

Tuesday, September 11, 2001, was a beautiful day in New York City, the Washington, D.C. area, and the Pennsylvania countryside. By the end of the day, the world had changed and would never be the same again. That morning, terrorist hijackers took control of four planes. Two were purposely crashed into the Twin Towers of the World Trade Center in New York City. Another was flown into the Pentagon, outside of Washington, D.C. Passengers attempted to retake control of the fourth hijacked aircraft, and it crashed into the Pennsylvania countryside. That plane's target will probably never be known with certainty.

As a result of the terrorist actions, thousands of people were killed, and a country was shaken to its core. Ten days after the attacks, the

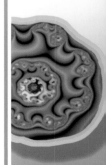

America: A Tribute to Heroes telethon and concert was held. Organized by actor George Clooney, the program raised money to help victims, families of victims, and rescue workers. More than $30 million dollars were raised to help those affected by the terrorist attacks.

Performers that evening came from almost every genre of the music industry. Bruce Springsteen, Neil Young, the Dixie Chicks, U2, Bon Jovi, and Mariah Carey were among those contributing their talents. So was Billy; he performed "New York State of Mind."

After the September 11, 2001, attacks on New York City's World Trade Center, Billy wanted to help those who had been affected by the devastating tragedy. Thousands had been killed, and Billy wanted to do something for those who had survived, as well as rescue personnel. On October 20, 2001, Billy joined other music stars for a benefit concert.

In October, another benefit concert was held, the Concert for New York City. Held at Madison Square Garden, the concert was organized by Paul McCartney. The audience was made up of mostly rescue workers and their families.

Again, the best of the music world performed. The Who, Mick Jagger, Melissa Etheridge, and Elton John were among those who lent their talents to the concert. So did Billy. He performed "New York State of Mind" and "Miami 2017 (Seen the Lights Go Out on Broadway)." After his performance, Billy addressed the crowd:

> **"I wrote that song ["Miami 2017 (Seen the Lights Go Out on Broadway)"] 25 years ago as a science fiction song never thinking it would be a reality, but unlike the end of that song, WE AIN'T GOIN' ANYWHERE!!"**

The crowd erupted into cheers and applause of agreement.

Dynamic Duo—Rocket Man and Piano Man

In the summer of 1994, Elton "Rocket Man" John and Billy toured together for the first time on the Face to Face tour. The piano duo appeared at stadiums in the United States and Canada, as well as some stops in Europe, Australia, and New Zealand. The tour made stops again in 1995 and 1998, and again in 2001, 2002, and 2003.

During the performances, Billy and Elton played each others songs. Then they joined each other for duets, much to the delight of the crowd. After a performance at San Diego University, one reviewer reflected on what he had just witnessed:

> **"They closed with 'Piano Man,' with Joel and John trading lyrics as the audience sang lyrics that have lived on longer than today's boy bands and Britney Spears fame combined. I had laughed at the age of the audience around me [most were middle aged] and my relative youthfulness, but then I wondered, as the smile ran away from my face, who my generation would go and see when the youth of today becomes the middle aged of tomorrow."**

Rocket Man meets Piano Man. In this photo taken before a concert in 2003, Elton John and Billy address the St. Louis, Missouri, crowd. The pair's Face to Face Tour has taken them all over the world, playing before huge crowds at each stop. It's a rare opportunity to see two music legends at once.

The concerts were more than just ways for Billy and Elton to pad their already-bulging pockets (though Elton has had some money problems). At various stops on the tours, the money from ticket sales went to charitable causes, including helping musicians in need.

Honors

During the early 2000s, Billy began to rack up honors for the work he did in and out of the recording studio. In 2001, Billy received the Johnny Mercer Award, the highest honor given by the Songwriters Hall of Fame. The award was created to honor a songwriter who has previously been inducted into the Songwriters Hall of Fame (Billy was inducted in 1992) and who has continued to establish a history of outstanding creative work.

In February 2002, Billy received the prestigious MusiCares Person of the Year Award. The award is presented to musicians who are also humanitarians. In announcing Billy's award, Michael Greene, President and CEO of the MusiCares Foundation and the Recording Academy said:

> **"Billy Joel's gift for lyric and melody rank him among the industry's most talented and accomplished musicians. He is a living symbol for what the Recording Academy stands for—his musical accomplishments are matched only by his endeavors as an advocate for music education. We truly are privileged to be honoring this gifted human being."**

In 2003, *Rolling Stone* magazine honored Billy's album *The Stranger*. The album was ranked #67 on the magazine's list of the 500 Greatest Albums of All Time. On September 20, 2004, Billy received a star on the famous Hollywood Walk of Fame in Los Angeles, California.

A Different Venue

Billy has never been afraid to try anything new. And in 2002, he again ventured into new waters—Broadway theater. Under the watchful and talented eye of famed choreographer Twyla Tharp, Billy put together some of his songs to create the musical *Movin' Out*. The musical tells the story of kids growing up in Long Island during the 1960s and how the Vietnam War affects them.

Movin' Out wasn't like ordinary musicals; it was more like a dance performance. The musical was basically a series of dances tied together by the barest of plots. And instead of the leads singing and speaking, all of the songs were performed by a pianist and band suspended above the stage.

The musical opened at the Richard Rodgers Theatre on October 24, 2002. In 2003, it was nominated for ten Tony Awards. It won two, one for Best Choreography and one for Billy and Stuart Malina for Best Orchestrations. On December 11, 2005, after more than 1,303 performances at the Richard Rodgers Theatre, the show closed.

Now fans can walk all over Billy when they visit Los Angeles, California. On September 20, 2004, Billy received a star on the Hollywood Walk of Fame—the 2,262nd celebrity to be so honored. The star is just one of the many honors to come to Billy in recognition of a long, successful career.

Musical theater wasn't the only different thing Billy tried in the early twenty-first century. Billy remarried in 2004. His bride, Katie Lee, a model and a host of Bravo's hit show *Top Chef*, was twenty-three, just a few years older than Alexa. He also tried his hand at writing. In 2004, he published a children's book, *Goodnight, My Angel*, which was

Billy's personal life has had its ups and downs: a stint in a psychiatric hospital, trips to rehab, multiple car accidents, and two divorces—including one from supermodel Christie Brinkley, the mother of his daughter Alexa Ray. But Billy wasn't ready to give up on marriage. In 2004, he married Katie Lee.

packaged with an audio CD. The book was basically an illustrated version of the lullaby he had written for Alexa. Many critics thought it was weak and too sentimental. Oh well, some things don't change.

Back Live

Billy began spring 2005 in rehab at the Betty Ford Clinic. He had also spent a brief time in rehab during 2002. He was drinking too much and too often, and he wanted to get his problem under control. Not long after Billy completed his treatment program, Columbia Records decided it was time to release another album. Fans were treated to a box set titled *My Lives.* The set is mostly demos, B-sides, and alternative versions of songs that were previously released. But there was something special about this particular set. It came with software that allowed people to mix their own versions of some of the songs, including "Only the Good Die Young" and "Keepin' the Faith," on their PCs.

In January 2006, Billy showed the world that he wasn't ready to stop touring. And fans weren't ready to have him stop touring; he sold out an unprecedented twelve concerts at New York City's Madison Square Garden. He didn't have any new material to play; the playlist contained a retrospective selection of his many hits and misses during his long career.

Billy also toured the United Kingdom and Ireland in 2006, his first performances there in several years. On July 31, 2006, Billy delighted thousands of fans in Rome, Italy, with a free concert of some of his greatest hits. An estimated 500,000 people enjoyed the outdoor concert.

In late 2006, Billy took his tour to South Africa, Australia, Japan, and Hawaii. As 2007, began, Billy was still touring, but he made an important stop on February 4, 2007 to sing the National Anthem before the kick-off of Super Bowl XLI. Billy had sung the National Anthem for Super Bowl XXIII. With the February 2007 performance, Billy became the first person to sing the National Anthem for two Super Bowls.

Billy and Music Education

Billy fell one English credit short of graduating from high school back in 1967. Twenty-five years later, the school board decided to waive the

English requirement in his case and awarded him a diploma during the 1992 graduation ceremonies.

The fact that Billy didn't graduate from high school—at least not as a traditional student—doesn't mean that he feels school isn't important. In fact, the opposite is true. And Billy has spent much of his time on projects supporting music education in schools. In times of tight budgets, the arts are often the first programs whose budgets are cut or even eliminated. To help raise awareness of the importance of music education, Billy has donated instruments and money to programs.

For a high school dropout, Billy has received his share of honorary college degrees. In this photo, Billy receives an Honorary Doctorate of Fine Arts from Syracuse University in 2006. The honors recognize his place as a music legend, of course, but they are more in recognition of his contributions to music education.

But his interest in musical education doesn't stop at the high school or grade school levels. He supports college music programs as well, teaching master classes at colleges all around the world. He established the Rosalind Joel Scholarship for the Performing Arts at City College in New York in honor of his mother. In 2005, Billy established the Billy Joel Endowment Fund. The fund will provide seed money, music scholarships, and endowments to colleges on the East Coast.

The Joel Legacy

In 2006, the world found out that Billy wasn't the only musically inclined Joel. As Billy Joel's only child, Alexa had been exposed to music all her life. She studied piano—including the classical composers—from an early age. Her skills as a songwriter also developed during her childhood. In 2006, Alexa became the first unsigned, independent artist to have a recording for sale at Target department stores when they agreed to carry *Sketches*. The success of the recording there convinced independent record stores to have it available for sale.

Alexa spent much of 2006 performing at college campuses in the Northeast. She also toured as part of the Hard Rock Café tour. Some music writers believe it's only a matter of time before she and her famous father perform together.

Billy Joel has been a fixture on the music scene for more than thirty-five years. During that time, he has proven that it is possible to have a successful career despite the critics. But in addition to his work as a musical artist, Billy is also working to keep music in the schools, to keep it a part of everyone's lives.

1949   **May 9** William Martin Joel is born.

1966   Billy joins a rock group called the Hassles.

1967   The Hassles release its first album, *The Hassles.*

   Billy, short just one credit, drops out of high school.

1969   The Hassles break up, and Billy and Jon Small for Atilla; the duo breaks up shortly after.

1971   Billy signs with Family Productions and releases his first solo album.

1972   Billy moves to California and begins a brief career as a lounge act.

1973   Billy signs with Columbia Records and *Piano Man* is released.

1975   Billy moves back to New York.

1977   *The Stranger* becomes Billy's first megahit.

1978   *The Stranger* brings Billy his first two Grammy wins.

   52nd Street becomes the first of Billy's albums to reach #1 on the album charts.

1979   *52nd Street* brings Billy two more Grammys.

1980   *Glass House* is Billy's second #1 album and brings him another Grammy.

1983   *An Innocent Man* is a huge success; a video for the album features Christie Brinkley, whom he marries in 1985.

1985   *Greatest Hits Vols. 1 & 2* is released and will be certified double diamond in 1999.

1986   **January 1** Daughter Alexa Ray Joel is born.

1987   **June** Billy becomes the first American rock star to perform in the USSR since the construction of the Berlin Wall.

1988   Billy voices a character and provides a song for the sound track of *Oliver and Company.*

1990   **June 22 and 23** Billy becomes the first rock act to perform a concert at Yankee Stadium.

1991 Connecticut's Fairfield University awards Billy an honorary doctorate; he would go on to receive several more.

1992 Billy receives a Grammy Living Legend Award.

Billy is inducted into the Songwriters Hall of Fame.

1994 **December 7** Billy receives a *Billboard* Century Award.

Billy and Elton John embark on the first Face to Face tour.

1995 Long-time bassist for Billy, Doug Stegmeyer, commits suicide.

1996 Billy takes a break from touring to lecture about classical music at colleges across the country.

1999 Billy is inducted into the Rock and Roll Hall of Fame.

2001 Billy's work as a classical composer is released as *Fantasies & Delusions.*

Billy receives the Johnny Mercer Award from the Songwriters Hall of Fame.

September 21 Billy performs on the *America: A Tribute to Heroes* telethon.

October Billy participates in the Concert for New York City.

2002 **February** Billy receives the MusiCares Person of the Year Award.

October 24 *Movin' Out,* a play written by Billy, opens on Broadway.

2003 *Movin' Out* is nominated for ten Tony Awards, winning two.

2005 Billy establishes the Billy Joel Endowment Fund to help college music programs.

2006 **January 7** Billy Joel's twelve sellouts at Madison Square Garden are acknowledged.

Billy kicks off a tour of South Africa, Australia, and Japan.

2007 Billy becomes the first artist to sing the National Anthem before two Super Bowls.

Albums

1971	*Cold Spring Harbor*
1973	*Piano Man*
1974	*Streetlife Serenade*
1976	*Turnstiles*
1977	*The Stranger*
1978	*52nd Street*
1980	*Glass Houses*
1981	*Songs in the Attic*
1982	*The Nylon Curtain*
1983	*An Innocent Man*
1985	*Greatest Hits, Vols. 1 & 2*
1986	*The Bridge*
1987	*KOHUEPT*
1989	*Storm Front*
1993	*River of Dreams*
1997	*Greatest Hits, Vol. 3; The Complete Hits Collection: 1973–1997*
2000	*2000 Years: The Millennium Concert*
2001	*Billy Joel—The Ultimate Collection; The Essential Billy Joel*
2002	*3 Pak: Piano Man, 52nd Street, KOHUEPT; 3 Pak: The Bridge, Storm Front, The Nylon Curtain*
2004	*Piano Man: The Very Best of Billy Joel; The Collection: Piano Man, 52nd Street, KOHUEPT*
2005	*My Lives*
2006	*12 Gardens Live*

Number-One Singles

1978	"Just the Way You Are"
1980	"It's Still Rock and Roll to Me"; "Don't Ask Me Why"
1983	"Tell Her About It"; "An Innocent Man"
1984	"The Longest Time"; "Leave a Tender Moment Alone"
1987	"This Is the Time"
1989	"We Didn't Start the Fire"
1993	"The River of Dreams"

Videos

1976 *Billy Joel Tonight*

1987 *Live from Leningrad*

1998 *Greatest Hits, Vol. 3*

2000 *Live at Yankee Stadium*

2001 *A&E Special: In His Own Words*; *Billy Joel—The Essential Video Collection*

2003 *Rock Masters: Billy Joel*

2007 *I Go to Extremes*

Books

2004 Joel, Billy. *Goodnight My Angel: A Lullabye*. New York: Scholastic.

2005 Joel, Billy. *New York State of Mind*. New York: Scholastic.

Select Awards/Recognition

1978 Grammy Awards: Song of the Year (for "Just the Way You Are), Record of the Year (for "Just the Way You Are).

1979 Grammy Awards: Best Pop Vocal Performance, Male (for *52nd Street*), Album of the Year (for *52nd Street*).

1980 Grammy Award: Best Rock Vocal Performance, Male (for *Glass Houses*).

1992 Grammy Awards: Lifetime Achievement Award; Billy is inducted into the Songwriters Hall of Fame.

1994 *Billboard*: Awards Billy a Century Award.

1999 RIAA: Certifies *Greatest Hits Vols. 1 and 2* double diamond; Billy is inducted into the Rock and Roll Hall of Fame.

2001 Songwriters Hall of Fame: Gives Billy the Johnny Mercer Award.

2002 MusiCares: MusiCares names Billy its Person of the Year.

2003 *Rolling Stone*: Ranks *The Stranger* #67 on its list of the 500 Greatest Albums of All Time.

Tony Awards: Wins for Best Orchestrations for *Movin' Out* (with Stuart Malina).

2004 Receives a star on the Hollywood Walk of Fame.

2006 Madison Square Garden recognizes Billy's twelve sellouts.

Books

Bego, Mark. *Billy Joel: The Biography*. New York: Thunder's Mouth Press, 2007.

Bordowitz, Hank. *Billy Joel: The Life and Times of an Angry Young Man*. New York: Watson-Guptill, 2005.

Geller, Debbie, and Tom Hibbert. *Billy Joel: An Illustrated Biography*. New York: McGraw-Hill, 1985.

Scott, Richard. *Billy Joel: All About Soul*. New York: Vantage, 2000.

Smith, Bill. *Piano Man: The Billy Joel Story*. New York: Book Republic Press, 2008.

Whitburn, Joel. *The Billboard Book of Top 40 Hit, 8th Edition*. New York: Billboard Books, 2004.

Web Sites

www.askmen.com/men/entertainment_150/173_billy_joel.html
Men of the Week: Billy Joel

www.billboard.com/bbcom/bio/index.jsp?pid=4939
Billy Joel on *Billboard*

www.billyjoelfan.com
Billy Joel Fan Site

www.rockhall.com
Rock and Roll Hall of Fame

www.rollingstone.com/artists/billyjoel/biography
Billy Joel on *Rolling Stone*

www.sonymusic.com/artists/BillyJoel
Billy Joel on Sony

audit—A formal examination of financial accounts.

calypso—Caribbean dance music that has syncopated rhythms, is usually improvised, and is often played by a steel band.

diverse—Very different of distinct from one another.

eluded—Escaped or avoided.

genres—Categories of artistic works.

gold—A designation that an album or CD has sold 500,000 units.

headline—To be the main attraction.

inductees—People formally admitted to an organization.

mastering—Creating an original copy of something from which other copies can be made.

mento—Jamaican music based on a folk dance rhythm.

New Wave—Rock music made in the late 1970s after the end of the punk era.

psychedelic—Relating to the effects of mind-altering drugs.

punk—A youth movement of the 1970s, characterized by loud rock music, confrontational attitudes, body piercing, and unconventional hairstyles, makeup, and clothing.

repertoire—The entire body of works for an artist.

retrospect—Reviewing the past from a new perspective or with new information.

underground—Separate from a prevailing social or artistic environment.

venues—Performance locations.

vintage—Classic, being of high quality and lasting appeal.

Ethan Schlesinger is a freelance author living in New York.

Picture Credits

page

2: Brian Zak/GAMMA
8: Kevin Mazur/WireImage
11: Kevin Mazur/WireImage
12: Kevin Mazur/WireImage
14: Columbia Records/NMI
17: Columbia Records/NMI
18: United Artists Records/KRT
20: Family Productions/NMI
23: Star Photo Archive
25: Columbia Records/NMI
27: Columbia Records/NMI
28: New Millennium Images
30: Columbia Records/PRNPS

32: New Millennium Images
35: Columbia Records/NMI
37: Foto Feature Collection
38: Star Photo Archive
41: New Millennium Images
43: Feature Photo Service
44: UPI Photo Service
47: Miami Herald/KRT
49: UPI Photo Service
51: Abaca Press/KRT
52: Columbia Records/PRNPS
54: Feature Photo Service

Front cover: Kevin Mazur/WireImage

FFR 2 2 2008

YA 782.42166 J591S
Schlesinger, Ethan.
Billy Joel /